Rebecca Hood

Palm

Reading

for Beginners

A Complete Guide for Palmistry. Learn How to Read your Palm and Discover your Destiny through the Art of Chiromancy

Table of Contents

PALMISTRY

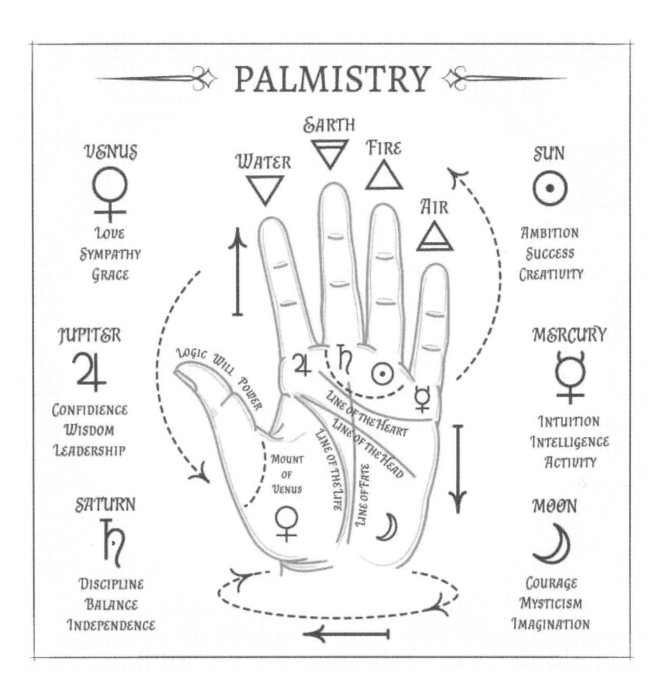

VENUS
Love
Sympathy
Grace

JUPITER
Confidence
Wisdom
Leadership

SATURN
Discipline
Balance
Independence

WATER

EARTH

FIRE

AIR

SUN
Ambition
Success
Creativity

MERCURY
Intuition
Intelligence
Activity

MOON
Courage
Mysticism
Imagination

Logic Will Power

Line of the Heart
Line of the Head
Line of the Life
Line of Fate

Mount of Venus

Palm Reading

Palm reading, palmistry, or palmistry as it is often called, is essentially the art of determining a person's character and predicting future events in a person's life by carefully studying their palm.

This practice occurs in a variety of forms in all cultures of the world. Those who practice Palmistry are usually referred to as palm or hand readers.

Many different, sometimes contrasting interpretations of different lines and other characteristics of the palm can be found in different schools of palm.

The length and shape of the lines on the palm, such as the heart and waist lines, etc., as well as the shape and size of the carriers or strikes offer different interpretations depending on their relative size, common qualities, intersections, and relationships with each other. In some palm reading traditions, players also take into account the properties of a person's fingers, fingerprints, and nails, as well as dermatoglyphs (leather models), skin color and texture, the overall shape of the palm, and the flexibility of the person's hand.

The reader will start by reading the person's dominant hand, in other words, the hands that the person uses the most or writes with. This hand is often seen as the hand representing the conscious mind, while the other hand represents the unconscious. Some traditions of reading palms I believe that this hand is familiar or hereditary traits. According to cosmological beliefs, when reading from the palm of a person, this hand can also transmit information about karmic or past life conditions.

The classical palm reading, a tradition that is most often used and taught, is essentially rooted in Greek mythology. According to this tradition, each part and area of the fingers and palm refers to a particular God or goddess, and the special characteristics of each area indicate the nature of the relevant aspects related to the subject. For example, the characteristics of a person's ring associated with Apollo relate to a person's relationship with aesthetics, art, fame, harmony, music, and wealth.

The meaning of each hand is discussed between different schools for palm reading, but it is usually assumed that the left hand detects potential within the person, and the right hand detects existing traits. In General, many palm reading experts agree that the left hand is for the past and the right for the future, although ultimately the choice of hand to use depends on each reader's individual attitude, experience, and instinct.

From a scientific point of view, the left hand is known to be controlled by the right half of the brain, which controls shape recognition and understanding of relationships. It is believed to reflect the inner personality, soul, or natural self and lateral thinking. Considered as part of personal and spiritual development, it is a feminine and receptive element of the Yin personality.

The right hand is known to control the left half of the brain, which is responsible for language, logic, and mind-it reflects the " I " in the objective, external person and the influence of education, experience, and social environment. It actually represents linear thinking and corresponds to the masculine aspects of "Yang" that come from the person's personality.

Among all the diverse and complex forms of divination as a way to predict the events of the future is palm reading one of the most basic, but most interesting forms. Formally called "palmistry", palm reading is the study of patterns on the inner side, to predict future events or foreshadow things not yet past.

The roots of palm reading go back more than 5,000 years in India, where Hindu sages and Roman fortune tellers (Gypsies) practiced art based on astrological principles. The practice eventually gained popularity, and quickly spread to other parts of Asia and Europe, including China, Tibet, Egypt, Persia and Greece.

The way palm reading works is that all the lines on your hand are designated and arranged into specific categories, for example "heart line" and "life line". The reader begins by examining the dominant hand of the subject and correlates the patterns on the hands of people to these categories.

To a large extent based on Greek mythology, the implications of how specifically organized lines appear on your hand correspond to a Greek god or goddess, who each represents some sort of theme or emotion. For example, the god Apollo resides in the annular of the hand of the entity that represents the themes of artistic, musical skills, skills, aesthetics, glory, wealth and harmony.

Other aspects of palm reading pay attention to other side properties such as size, skin color and nails. These characteristics are again organized, as well as the model line, into 10 categories that are largely based on elementary theory. For example, if you realize that you have a "fire hand" (identified as a hand with a square palm, reddened skin, short fingers), their personality should reflect a high level of energy, creativity, ambition, and sometimes choleric.

Other identifiable features on the hand can be interpreted as "Earth hand", seen through the palm and square fingers, and rough skin, which is darker and more turbid in color," air hand "seen through rectangular palms, long fingers, prominent knuckles and dry skin, or" water hand", which is seen through the palm and square fingers.

As for the scientific validity of palm reading, many scientists questioned the practice, which were identified as having little or no significant scientific principles. Many reject the legitimacy of palm reading based on this fact, and also because it can be classified in the culture of "cold reading". That is, palm reading is widely used by the culture of people who claim to have psychic abilities, but only for profit. This kind of false practice implies that palm reading is too big a thing to take it seriously. However, other studies suggest that some of the astrological principles that coincide with the symbols on your hand would produce an interesting analysis that does not focus on the physical body and psychological mind, but rather scientific.

The complexity behind the practice of palm reading are often overlooked, so once attention is removed from the supernatural, some of the astrological characteristics or principles in the art of palm reading could produce important scientific results.

PALM READING IS USED IN VARIED FORMS AROUND THE WORLD

The practice of reading in the palm of the hand, also known as palmistry or palmistry, is found all over the world. There are a number of cultural variations that are primarily aimed at the same goal. It is essentially a method for assessing certain character traits and current circumstances, as well as for understanding the likelihood of future events.

Guessing palm as a method of divination has very ancient roots that come from different cultures. Historically, many agree that this practice comes from Hindu astrology in India and then developed in China and other Asian countries.

From there it is believed that it has been expanded and improved in the Middle East and finally in Europe. Today, many think primarily about the Gypsy Gypsies associated with Palmistry. In fact, they did not adopt the craft as a way to predict the fate much later than some other cultures.

Manual analysts often combine their art with various other divination techniques. Some use it in combination with astrology, numerology or some other kind of prediction system. It is not uncommon when combined with tarot cards or other reading cards. Of course, many palm readers rely on only one system to provide observations and forecasts.

In both cases, reading in the palm of your hand involves assessing a person's character or predicting the likelihood of future events by looking at that person's Palm. The reader interprets functions such as lines, projections, shapes and other functions to make observations and predictions.

Depending on the specific background of the player, you can consider the texture of the skin, the color of the hand or the size of the hand. The flexibility, thickness or length of the fingers can also occur depending on the variety of palm used. There are many techniques that are actively practiced and each specific reading will depend on the specific history of the reader.

However, the emphasis on the lines on the palm is almost universal for all forms of Palm. Most people know what is called the lifeline. This is considered for such features as the length and general position on the palm. Other factors include curves or straightness and whether they intersect with other significant lines.

In addition to the life line, the head line and the heart line are the main indicators that are usually analyzed. The head line is usually considered an idea of how the human mind can function, while the heart line will focus on physical and emotional problems. While some people think that the Lifeline is how long you will live, it is most often used as an indicator of how you lived and how you live.

Sometimes there is a debate on the page to read. Some customs show that the left hand shows the potential of a person, and the right hand shows the realized personality. Some say that the future is displayed in the right hand, and the past on the left. Others argue that the right hand of a man should read and the left hand of a woman. Finally, the decisive factor is the method that best suits the reader.

A Brief Insight into Palm Reading

Palmistry is also called Palm Reading. It is about telling about the future and character of a person by reading the lines in the palm of a person's hand. The origins of palm reading are the ancient astrology of India.

The structure of a person's palm speaks of a person's personality. A person whose palm structure is soft is known to be sensitive; and if the texture is rough, the person is allegedly violent. If a person's hand is flexible, it is said to be an adjustable person in any environment. If the fingers are elastic, they say that there is a person who is ready to cope with problems. Human nails also speak about a person's personality. If a person has long nails that are pointed at the end, the person is allegedly creative. If he has short nails, he must be very organized. The color of the palms has nothing to do with astrology. But if a person's hand is pink, they say that it has good health.

The parts that rise under the toes are known as the palm hill. The study of these reefs is called chirognomy. Mountains play a significant role in Palmyra. Some of the functions associated with handles are as follows:

* The person who goes down the mountain Jupiter is ambitious, loves nature, and leadership qualities.

* Man goes down the slope of Saturn, stern, burning, and has wisdom.

* A person walking down the slope of the Apollo has intelligence, works well, and is an artist.

* A person who goes down the slope of mercury is flat-headed, business-minded, and also selfish.

* A person who descends from mount Venus has qualities such as passion, compassion, and love.

* The person who goes down the hill the Moon is cold, resourceful and selfish.

The palm is very important when reading from the palm of your hand. The three most important lines are the Heart line, the lifeline, and the main line. The heart line shows the emotional characteristics of a person. In addition, he also discusses issues related to the heart and personal relationships. The area where the heart line begins indicates a personal inclination to love. The shape and length of the line are related to sensations.

The lifeline is a human life. In addition, it also talks about the nature and potential human health problems.

The way the curved lifeline is in the palm of your hand is a sign of how a person manages their life, as well as proof of health. The length will tell you how many people will survive.

The main role is related to intelligence. This is also related to psychological and mental problems that a person may have in their life. The distance from the head to the heart line indicates a person's happiness and happiness. It is also a line that can speak to human memory.

There are additional lines on the palm used to read from the palm, and include the double line, the glory line, and the Venus belt.

Palm Reading Guide

Reading in the palm of your hand is a great way to understand Palmistry on a deeper level and get the best results. Palmistry dates back to antiquity and is still practiced all over the world, revealing many mysteries.

I encourage you to discover the secrets that are in our left and right hands. It is amazing that so much of our past, present and future are revealed through this ancient form of divination.

This is something that you can discover and help you understand the meaning that lies within the head, waist, belt of Venus, the sun and, most importantly, the line of destiny in our hands. The best way to discover and understand these secrets is to find a reading guide in the palm of your hand.

You will learn how the left hand gives us information about our relationships, it also reflects our inner confidence and, most importantly, our spiritual and personal growth in life. Your right hand reflects the aspect of yourself, your observations and the influence of the people around you, your education, etc., experiences. There are so many information to know the shape, the color, skin texture and even our fingernails, all of this will help us to understand and connect with ourselves in a way that is new and wonderful.

Many of us have different hand shapes, but thanks to reading in the palm of your hand, there is so much to learn about the shape of our hands, for example; is the shape of your hand a sign of Earth, air, water or fire? All this is taken into account when reading palm lines that can tell us many aspects of our life and answer many questions we want to know, such as: will I be famous? How many children will I have? Can I do that? Can I find my soul? Am I going to travel? Am I going to write a book?

You will find new causes and goals by learning the meaning of the mountains of the Moon, Venus, Mars, Jupiter, Saturn, Sun, Mercury, Mars, Rach and keth. Each will have a meaningful meaning that can change the way you look at your life and channel the changes you need to make. Revealing the secrets that are in the palm of your hand, you'll be able to make so many positive changes in your life, that has given me so much confidence, strength and positive influence to follow the ambitions that I until I have them in the palm of my hand.

I highly recommend you to discover the many mysteries and riddles about yourself contained in your hands, reading in the palm of your hand is a great way to get an idea and answer so many questions! There are many palm reading guides to help you answer questions if you are new to palm reading or want to read palm trees.

Palm Reading For Beginners

Palm reading, also known as Palmistry or Palmistry, is a fascinating way to predict your future by learning the palm of your hand.

Returning to Hindu astrology and Roma traditions, Palm reading is currently practiced all over the world.

HAND SHAPE

Most Palm readers use a person's dominant or more active hand to read. When you define the dominant hand, the palmist will analyze some qualities of the palm. The first is the shape of the hand itself. There are four common types of hands that fit the elements:

Fiery hands are long palms of square or rectangular shape with short fingers. These people usually leave and want to be under control. Usually they are strong and angry.

Airy hands-square palm with long fingers several times accompanied by dry skin. Such people tend to be cheerful and enjoy intellectual stimulation. They communicate well and love to write.

Water hands are long rectangular palms with long fingers. Emotional and expressive, these people tend to make great musicians and poets.

Terrestrial hands are square palms with short fingers. People with earthly hands tend to enjoy life in the fresh air. They are stable people who do not like change. You can find many artists with earthly hands.

PALM LINES

Palms usually use four wide lines or wrists on the palm to predict the future: fate, heart, life and head lines. Each line defines a different aspect of their personality and future life.

Line of Destiny - the line of destiny is below the index. A strong line of Destiny predicts a stable person. The weak line of fate belongs to those who often change jobs. The lack of a line of Destiny means that a person lacks stability in their lives.

Heart line-the heart line appears at the top of the palm, under the fingers. This line represents all areas of the heart, including love life, their emotional stability, novels and even heart health.

Waist-this line is located on the edge of the palm above the thumb and extends over a semicircle to the wrist. This line does not represent human longevity. Palmists believe that this line represents the physical health, vitality and strength of a person. The life line also reflects great changes and events in life.

Head line-the head line starts at the edge of the palm under the viewfinder and passes through the palm. This line represents how a person thinks. It defines a person's learning style, attitude to creative or analytical learning methods and style of communication.

WHAT IS THE SIMIAN LINE?

The Simian line is another large palm line. Not everyone has a prominent Simian line. For those who do, this interesting line crosses the palm, replacing the line of the heart and head. Some palmists believe emotionally, and reasoning can be learned with this line alone. It is also believed that those who have a Simian line never find inner peace. They tend to see things only in black or white, without shades of gray. Thus, you can find out that the Simian line means constant tension in his life.

While many believe they read pseudoscience, others swear only on their reality and base their lives on their research. Look at the palm of your hand and determine how accurate the statements on the palm reading are. Perhaps there is a reason why this ancient practice is still in use today.

WHAT YOU CAN GET OUT OF A PALM READING EXPERIENCE

The ancient art of palm reading is known as a way to predict future events ahead by studying the features of a person's Palm. Another name for this technique is palmistry. The history of palm reading goes back to the Greek philosopher Aristotle, although it is possible that the technique began elsewhere, such as the ancient Roman Empire, or in China or India. Today, palm reading is practiced in many places around the world. There are people who read palm trees in one form or another on all continents. People who practice this ancient art can be called palmists or manual analysts.

The hand of each person consists of seven main areas, which in palmistry are called supports. Vectors represent certain characteristics associated with planetary influences. The palm of the hand is a record of a person's life that describes in detail where we have been and what challenges may come in the future. Palm reading can be used as a way to understand your life from a deeper point of view. The mountains are also divided into seven colors of the rainbow and help the palm tree to know what the problems in our lives are right now and what is happening in the future. Here are the seven carriers and what they represent:

Sun Mount shows your level of honesty and success in life. Mount Moon represents how you perceive and interact with the world. Mount Mercury is a measure of enlightenment and your responsibility. Mount Venus stretches from Mount Moon and talks about how we treat the physical world. Mars is a sign of the energy that passes through our body and how we use them. Mount Saturn is the understanding of our search for meaningful answers to the great questions of life. Keta and Rahu are read together in combination. Keta is a representation of the life choices we have drawn from our lives and how we have treated them. Rahu is a representation of our current environment and how it relates to our future.

There are three outstanding lines that lie on the hand of almost every person, and they are carefully examined by the analyst's hand. These lines are known as the heart line, the headline and the life line. These different lines are the expression of your life story and talk about your emotional, mental and physical health. The palms will read the palm headline to tell you about the life of your mind. The headline will show the style of thinking you are using. The heart line tells Palm Reader about your emotional health and physical health. The lifeline is perhaps the most controversial of them, because it reflects physical health and constantly changing life events.

Be sure to contact us if you would like more information about palm reading and if you want to know what the palm of your life says. We can assure you that we will help you understand palm reading and know the benefits that this knowledge can bring you.

Palmistry or Chiromancy

Palmistry, also known as chiromancy, is the practice of foretelling the future of a person, by careful study and observation of the lines and other characteristics of the palm. Palmistry has existed as a method of predicting the future, for over a thousand years. There are notable studies and scripts on palmistry found in ancient Hindu mythology, Chinese astrology and even Gypsy fortune telling. Thus, we can safely assume that it has existed across cultures and since a very long time.

Somewhere in the Middle Ages, under the pressure from the Catholic Church, the practice of palmistry was suppressed and even deemed a hoax. However, around 1839, it was revived by palmist and author Captain Casimir Stanislas D'Arpentigny's publication on the subject, called 'La Chirognomie'.

In the current world, Palmistry is a well-known and followed belief. Although there are a lot of people who do not consider it authentic since it is not supported by scientific evidence, the believers hold it to be highly revealing. Scientists have also claimed the idea to be misleading because the constant movement of the palm and use of fingers leads to fine lines forming throughout.

Like most concepts in astrology, palmistry too has certain symbols and signatures that are used to predict or foretell.

1. Hand Shape:

There are four types of hand shapes recognized in palmistry, namely Earth, Air, Water and Fire.

• Earth - Broad, square palms and fingers. Thick, coarse skin. Length of palm, from wrist to base of the finger, is equal to length of the fingers.

• Air - Rectangular palms and fingers with knuckle protruding. Thumbs are low set and length of the palm is equal to that of the fingers.

• Water - Long, oval shaped palms, with long fingers. The length of the palm from wrist to base of fingers is usually less, than the length of fingers.

• Fire - Square or Rectangular palms, with shorter fingers. Length of the palm from wrist to finger base is usually greater, than the fingers.

Once the shape of the palm is determined, the next stage involves examining the lines of the fingers. These lines are said to be indicators of the different facets and stages of a person's life. Guess it's safe to say, shape matters!

2. Lines:

There are four major lines found on almost all palms and are considered the major lines.

• Heart Line - It represents the love and attraction or human relationships. It runs from the end of the palm, below the little finger, across the palm. It deals with the emotional life. Apart from romantic perspectives it also talks of a person's ability to deal with emotions.

So a person with a chained heart line is said to be emotionally unstable. If the line is clear and well set, the person is supposed to be having good emotional stability.

• Head Line - It runs from the end of the palm, between the thumb and the index finger, below the heart line. It represents a person's mind and the way his thoughts work.

This includes learning ability, learning style, working style, intellectual prowess and all other mental capabilities (tells you if you are thinking straight!).

• Life Line - It flows from between the thumb and the index finger and moves downward to the edge of the palm, ending above the wrist. It slopes downward, creating a separate section for the mound at the base of the thumb. It reveals a person's vitality, vigor, general well-being, etc.

Earlier it was believed to be an indicator of the length of a person's life. However modern palmistry discounts the idea (Thank God for that!) and says that it only deals with the aspects of life and not the longevity.

• Fate Line - It runs from the base of the palm, starting from the wrist and cuts through the heart line and head line, moving upwards. It is sometimes missing in some people's hands. As the name suggests, it indicates a person's fate, in respect of the life path he chooses.

In addition to the lines, there are also various other mounts and finer lines that are read for information. However the concept is one which is avoided in many practices on the pretext of being too ambiguous.

Some palmists read these lines, while others discount their importance. But the lines mentioned above are agreed to be the most important ones from the modern palmistry point of view.

Psychic and Palm Reading

So many facts about your life can show you reading the palm of your hand. When you look at your palm, each of these different lines in your hand will determine something interesting about you. If you are wondering about the future of your well-being, future well-being of your Bank account or future well-being of your loneliness, all you can see through the palm with a mental reading of your palm.

Reading from the palm of your hand may be easier than you think. There are many resources that teach the media how to give a palm reading. When you drive on the highway, you will most likely pass through a site that offers data from the palm of your hand. Even some centers have booths where the media offers information from the palm of their hand for five to ten dollars. Mental palm reading is a harmless mental reading that people usually choose. Many people are afraid of getting intense psychological data; however, they will only get mental palm reading for fun.

To read the media, you must remember that you have a choice whether you believe or not. Just because of a message or advice that provides you with safe media, it doesn't mean that you should live your life in fear that it will become a reality. For example, if your psychic palm reading shows that you never get married or live a miserable single life; don't believe that this turned out to be true. You can live your life with a new desire to find true love as a psychological palm reading. Who knows, you could prove your psychic palm reading completely wrong and end a happy family life in peace? Psychological data from the palms of your hands is usually cheaper than other psychological evidence.

This is another reason why people do this just for fun. It gives you a little piquancy of a boring life. It might not have been as much fun if you just read in the palm of your hand, but if you go there with a group of friends, it can translate to a pretty nice moment. Maybe the next time you can go with your group of friends to a fun night at the Mall, you should shoot it. Perhaps even one of your friends will have a big impact on their lives.

Some people are ashamed to pay money for psychological data and resort to calling it "stupid" even though they are secretly interested in doing so. If you are one of these people, you have hundreds of psychic palms to read books where you can even do basic palm reading in the privacy of your home. Palm reading books can be purchased at any bookstore. From the comfort of your bedroom or living room, you can do palm reading at your own pace, to my delight.

PSYCHIC PALM READING

The practice of reading on the palm goes back to prehistory. Roh's images also show that the hand is considered an important part of the body. For prehistoric humans, the hand would be one of the obvious benefits that distinguish them from the other animals that surround them. Later, when communication skills developed and understanding emerged, there were the first signs that we are learning palmistry. Palmistry seems to be the first time in India. The ancient letters relating to this practice have been preserved; the techniques used so far have been derived from these first works.

From its roots in India, the art of reading through the palm of the hand began to spread all over the world. As art moved from one country to another, the methods adapted to different cultures, their interpretations of its functioning and its spiritual and religious beliefs. In some cultures, the connection between palm reading and mental connection is clearly understood from the very beginning.

Aristotle wrote about reading on the palm of his hand, and there is other evidence that it is widely practiced in ancient Greece. During her travels, she said that

Alexander the Great returned to the birthplace of Palmistry to learn more about her. Perhaps he discovered the idea of connecting meaning and meaning in several lines. Whether true or not, palmistry seems to have certainly been used in one form or another along with other disciplines and practices of ancient Greece and other ancient civilizations. Examples of this are some evidence that Julius Caesar used it in Rome. Maybe he used a palm reading technique to decide if people are right for him or not.

In the Western world, palm trees frowned on the spread of Christianity. He became associated with Pagan and heretical practices, and anyone who used Palmistry risked being accused of witchcraft. So, the art went underground. But it remained popular in India and continued to grow there without the risk of harassment to its users. In fact, it is increasingly respected as a form of prediction of Fate. Gypsies brought him from India and gradually, thanks to his influence, became more common throughout Europe.

Today, Palmistry is widely practiced and there are many people who earn their living with their own practice and write books on how to read effectively, etc, There are actually many publications and web sites available if you are interested and want to know the meanings of the strings, how they interact, and how to read.

HOW IT DIFFERS FROM NORMAL PALM READINGS

If you are interested in knowing your future, you should go to the psychological data from the palms. Now the question is why you should look for this type of reading instead of the usual one. This is simply because clairvoyance is one of the very advanced, and offers more accurate information. Here in this article we will learn the main advantages of extrasensory reading in the palm of your hand and compare it with the usual one.

More Intuitive

When it comes to reading extrasensory palms, it means choosing someone with special psychic abilities. Reading can therefore be expected to be more insightful and support in-depth analysis. Media receive help from their innate mental abilities in the analysis of the palm, so their result is at least 90% accurate.

More Targeted

Psychic data from the palms will help you assess your future, so they will help you focus more on your future. When you focus on your future, you learn to grow and develop your plan accordingly. This will help you understand the obstacles that can hinder your growth in life.

More Loyal

When you ask for help from an experienced psychic, you can be sure that you have more reliable information, because only psychics can predict your life based on past and current events with their incredible intuitive powers. A normal psychic reader can superficially look at my life on the basis of the information available; however, the psychic reader examines the reality thanks to its ability to predict deeply.

How to Use Palm Reading To Create Instant Attraction with Beautiful Women

Many girls love things that are a kind of "new age" and mysticism. Of course, this doesn't work for all women, so you'll need to ease yourself into the game.

The first thing you need to do is learn a little about palm reading. Just learn the basics and different lines are spoken. Google is your friend.

So you need to go where he is, hold his hand and talk about your future. This is not an average company. You can't go in there and say, "Hey, it's Bob!" Give me your hand and I'll tell you about my future!"

Although it may work, you need to rest in it. This works best when with a group of friends. Once you get a lot of success with this in groups, you can start using it on single girls.

The best approach is to break down its state, the Preface is your introduction, and then ask for its permission. Now asking for permission doesn't put you in the "beta" field unless you are overly stressed. Be sure to express this as "fabric softener"."

Say something like this: "sorry, I couldn't help noticing. I know this will look incredibly strange to you, but ... .. it seems like you have a little bit of energy on you. In fact, you remind me of a girl who had a bright future. In fact, I have read the palm, and many of these things are true."

Opinions about a lot of things. First, it's a break. This will create curiosity. Also, you already say it's weird, so if it thinks you're weird, you've already said it, then it will look normal. Then you said you did it with the previous girl. This will take away any idea that this is some kind of pickup line.

Then when you describe a girl, you are incredibly vague. It will almost certainly be incredibly interesting. So if you're wondering if they want to read this palm tree, it's almost safe to say that.

Of course it's yours. List a few obvious things, and then ask her to comment, which she will be happy to give. Make sure she's calm. Compliment her on her "energy" and tell her that she has a bright future.

How do you want to shut up? Say something like this:

"Look, I don't know if you believe in fate or anything, but it was fun talking to you. I think you're a very interesting person. I would like to be with you later over a Cup of coffee or something like that. Give me your phone number to pick up the set."

Palm Reading Demystified

For many centuries, a person was mystified by the science of reading from the palm or palmistry. True, many people vainly tried to uncover the secret to reading palms and making fun of him in an attempt to prove it as a trash can. And yet over the years, nothing has happened to minimize the significance that palmistry has achieved in the mind of the common man.

On the other hand, was to study the features of the hand accidentally connected with black magic, errors and other superstitions that have gathered in the minds of the uninformed. These myths should be revealed in order to understand the seriousness and benefits of this great science for mankind. Let's look at the first five myths about palmistry that exist today and try to demystify them.

1. Palmistry can predict your future:

You can hear how people predict your life by simply looking at your hands-that is, they do not have complete knowledge of science. If someone says that your life will be short just because your life is short, stop panicking and give the Thorns a reflection. Palmistry, unlike common notion, is not a trick that foretells how many children you will have or reveal the spouse of your name. Divination actually shows current patterns and trends to better tell the natural search results. In the end, it is your thoughts and actions that determine what your future will be.

2. Manual analysis is disabled in the Bible:

It would be good to read the Holy Scripture and understand the meaning of words using practical biblical consensus. Although many like to play "banned by the church" wisdom, the fact remains that most Pope in the middle ages he showed interest in palmistry as well as astrology and alchemy. Even the first manuscripts from the palm were found in European monasteries, which support these revelations.

3. Your index predicts your spirituality:

In the palm of your hand, the index finger is an important sign of the body. It refers primarily to the authority, ambition and ego of a human being. These are by no means symbols that represent the spirituality of man. In short, the human index can not reveal the depth of a person's sacred and religious ideas.

4. There is no scientific basis for palmistry:

No other myth can be further from the truth. The lines of your hand represent a graphic image of the circuits in your brain. The nerve groups that control your hand are located in the epicenter of the brain, which is why palmistry is a great success.

5. Prehistoric cultures practiced palmistry:

Although most people like to support this theory, there are no real facts to support such a theory. We can speculate on this topic, because there is nothing left of our ancestors about palmistry.

Today, palmistry is one of the most famous Sciences in the world. Understanding the science of palmistry will help you better arm yourself against such mythical mistakes.

Main And Small Hands

Each of us has two hands described as Main and smaller hands in palmistry. The main hand is the one you use most naturally. If you're right, it'll be your right hand. Of course, it will be the left hand if you are left-handed.

Traditionally, the main page was the one that records what you do with your life, while a smaller hand reveals the skills, abilities and traits born of S. But even if there is a truth about it, it does not make the whole story.

Our hands change for life. Our little hands also change, and this will not happen if they simply show what we were born with. As a result, I believe that the main hand is to understand what the person is actually doing, while the smaller hand shows what the person is thinking about. It's always a map of potential, but it changes to reflect what the person wants to do. Of course, this can be completely different from what a person does in his daily life.

As a result, both hands should be examined when reading the palm of the hand. When I read quickly, perhaps in a festive situation, I look only at the main hand. However, I always study both hands when giving a serious reading.

SKIN TEXTURE

It is easier to determine the texture of the skin of the face by looking at the back of the hand. The texture of the skin is the quality of the skin and can range from fine and smooth to rough and rough.

The texture of the skin shows how refined a person is. Someone with a very soft, silky and smooth skin, because the child will be sensitive, tender and refined in perspective. This person will easily be upset, which will affect his sensitivity.

On the other hand, a person with rough skin will be rougher, feet on the ground and less stressed than a person with a fine skin texture. This man will not simple and simple.

The texture of the skin gives you an immediate hint of how a person works in life. For example, it would be difficult to imagine someone with rough hands selling beautiful works of art. However, this person could sell Engineering shares.

CONSISTENCY

We can get a lot of information by contacting someone. The one who takes the hand with a firm grip conveys the best instant impression of someone offering a wet and inanimate hand.

Once the texture of the skin on the back of the hand is determined, turn the person's hands higher and gently press on the palms.

The consistency is determined by the degree of elasticity in the hand. The texture of the hand varies from extremely heavy to soft and spongy.

People with soft, spongy hands are sensual pleasure lovers who do as little work as possible. They work best in a comfortable environment where they can dream and lick their life.

People with stronger and more stable hands are practical, energetic and valuable. They love challenges and must be used to be happy.

FLEXIBILITY

The flexibility of the human mind is determined by the flexibility of the palm. People with flexible hands adapt and can quickly adapt to changing circumstances. People with hard hands are inflexible, stubborn and rigid.

To determine the flexibility of someone's hand, I lean on the back of the hand on the toes, pressing the thumb against the fingers. Some people have arms that feel like a piece of wood, while others have arms that bend and create almost the right angle. Most people have their hands somewhere between these two extremes.

COLOR

The color of the hand gives valuable clues about the health and temperament of a person. The colors of our hands change naturally depending on the temperature. People are likely to feel the cold when they have blue hands. Maybe they came in while they were out in the snow. However, there is a divination if the room temperature is normal, but the hands of a person have a bluish tinge.

For example, people with white hands are likely to be anemic. This leads to a lack of vitality and energy. These people are heartless and selfish. They become irritable and easily frustrated. They are autonomous, idealistic and cold.

Hands with a yellowish tinge belong to people who have a slightly sharp view of the world. Blue hands show that human blood is circulating.

He's poor.

Pink hands are considered normal in people of European origin. This is a good sign and shows that the person loves, is grateful, responds and supports.

Red hands belong to people with a lot of energy. It is important to use this energy wisely. People with red hands can easily lose nerves. Sometimes redness is visible only on one part of the arm. Once this happens, the energy of this particular case, returning to school, will only increase.

HAND SHAPE

There are several ways to order the hand, but it is certainly easier to determine whether the palm is square or rectangular in shape.

SQUARE PALM

People with the square palm are capable and practical. They take advantage of the challenges and are ready to work long and hard when it is necessary to achieve their goals. They have a lot of stamina and energy.

EXTENDED, PALM

Extended palms are hands that artists like. These arms are long and thin, but much less practical than a meter of arms. People with stretched palms like to come up with ideas, but they often remain dreams and rarely eat. These people are creative, idealistic and tender.

This divides the entire human race into two categories. We can double this by examining the fingers and classifying them as short or long. Usually it is enough to set short or long fingers in proportion to the palm of your hand. Sometimes, however, it can be difficult to make a decision. If so, ask the person to put his fingers in the palm of his hand. It is said that if the fingers reach more than seven octaves of the distance from the Palm, they are long. However, this is also not ideal, because some people have more flexible hands and fingers than others. If it is not possible to determine whether the long or short fingers are proportional to the palms, they clearly have an average length.

Short Fingers

People with short fingers quickly absorb and become impatient when people take all day. They like to get in, do the job and get out as quickly as possible. They like to be busy and often face many different tasks, all at once. In the beginning, they are often better than in the end. They prefer a wide and general appearance and do not appreciate the details.

Long Fingers

People with long fingers appreciate detailed and attractive work. They are patient and want to take all the time necessary to successfully fulfill the task. They like to finish what they start. Have the responsibility, accountability and love in order to cut down on the essence of things, to understand why they work.

Middle finger

Many people have fingers that are neither long nor short. These people are a mixture of qualities of people who have short and long fingers.

As a result, they can be patient, but impatient with others. Most are conscientious and responsible, but can work with a slash, if not for them the task too attractive.

Knowing the length of your finger can only be useful to you in everyday life. If you need to queue somewhere, try to choose a line waiting for the cashier with short fingers. The line of this person will move faster than the cashier with long fingers, who will want everything to check again. Cashier with short fingers will try to treat people as quickly as possible and take care of the settlement of the cashier at the end of the day.

However, there are cases when you want the person they are dealing with to pay special attention to the details. In this case, choose someone with the longest fingers you can find.

Classification of Hands

We now have four possible combinations: a square hand with short fingers, square hand with long fingers, elongated hand with short fingers and oblong hand with long fingers.

These four species can be combined with four elements: earth, air, fire and water.

HAND OF THE EARTH

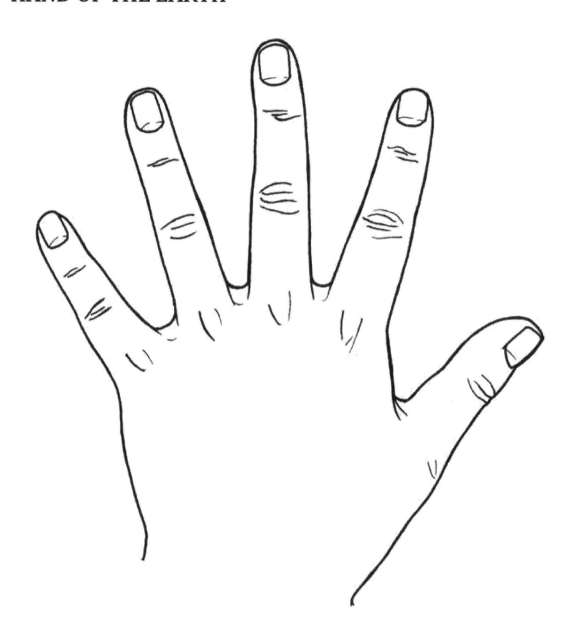

Hand, the Earth is a square hand with short fingers (the picture under the hands of a Country usually has several lines, although the lines are currently well-marked. Such people are always busy and like to do things with their own hands. They are practical, attentive, reliable and durable. However, they can also be impatient, suspicious, critical and easily awakened. They enjoy the outdoor life and prefer a quiet lifestyle, away from the hustle and bustle of big cities. They appreciate the importance of the country and somehow cooperate with the country. Usually they are stress-free and accept life exactly as it comes. This philosophy means that in general they have good health and lead a long and fruitful life.

AIR HAND

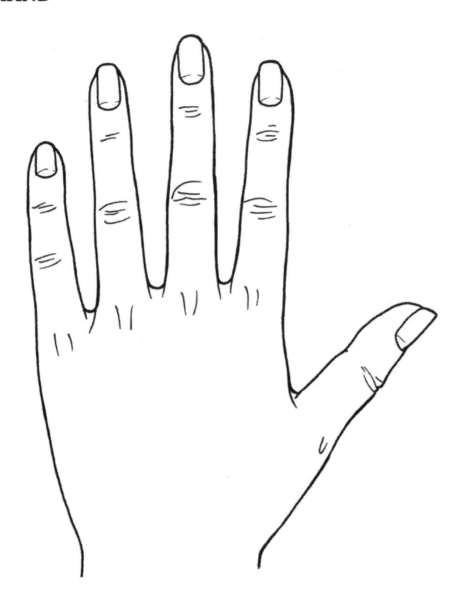

The air hand consists of a square palm and long fingers (photo below, these people are creative, innovative, practical and thoughtful. They are conscientious, know the details well and need constant problems. The air arm belongs to someone who is smarter than someone with an earthly arm. Despite this emphasis on intelligence, even people with airborne hands have a strong intuition.

They can quickly decide using a combination of logic and meaning. They like to express themselves, but just leave. They have a special nature, which always keeps them young. They are beautiful and well expressed. They are interested in travel, communication, freedom and everything that is a little out of order.

FIRE HAND

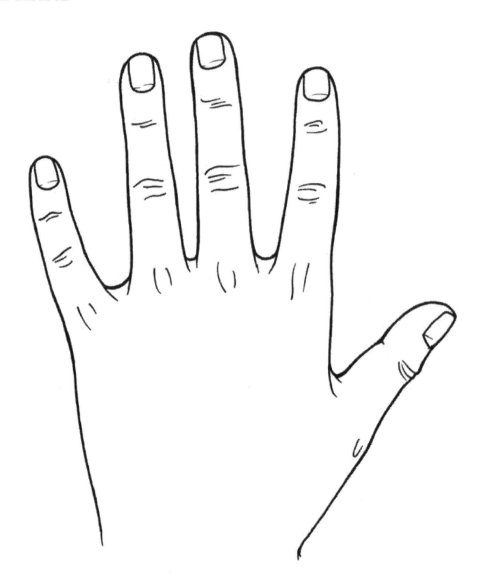

The burning arm consists of an elongated palm and short fingers. These people are excellent, enthusiastic, universal and impatient. They have great ideas, but they need to be carefully evaluated to make sure they are practical before you jump on them. They are better in wide touches than small details and often lose interest, before completing the task. Their volatile nature can sometimes upset others, but in general they are able to bring people with their energy and excitement. They are generous, sociable and sinful. Bouncers have to be busy to be happy. It will not take much time to work too simple, boring or boring.

WATER HAND

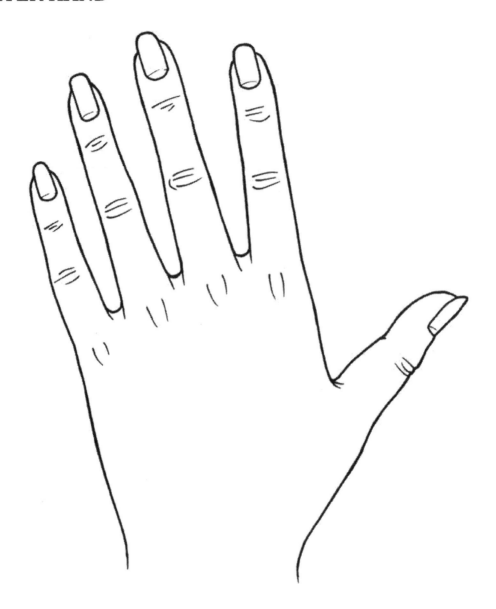

The water hand consists of an elongated palm and long fingers. This is a form that artists like, but in everyday life they are not very comfortable. People with water hands lead a rich emotional life and are extremely resourceful and sensitive. So succeed in any career, which includes creativity and a strong aesthetic significance. They are mostly idealists and constantly feel frustrated by human actions, and the hands are formed differently from their own. They are receptive, changeable and malleable. They are also warm and have a lot of love for all living things. This creates the impression of calm and control, but inside he suffers from nervous tension and fear.

This classification system manual is the most useful today, because all of them can be divided into four groups. D arpentigny system, which was developed in the last century, which was classified people into seven groups, however, is still used, and you will find it useful, about this Learn.

It was a system that originally taught me and I still mentally put people in one of those categories. However, the four-element classification system is what I basically use.

BASIC MANUAL

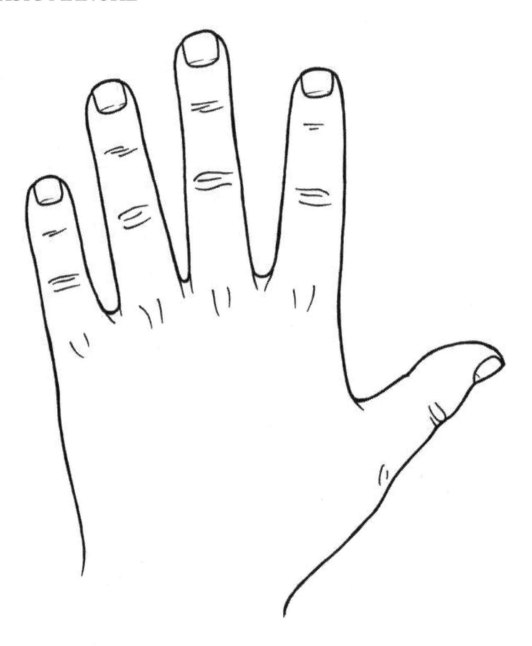

The main hand is a little clumsy. The palm is Square, and the fingers are short, short and relatively shapeless. The skin is rough, and the back of the hand is often soft. The palm consists of several lines, sometimes only two or three. These people are stubborn and hard to say. They take life as it comes, live today and make small plans for the future. These people are good hands, and sometimes they can be extremely creative.

This hand was often when D'arpentigny developed his system. He found a lot of peasants with basic hands. However, this type of hand has become even rarer, and in practice, the basic right hand is rarely found.

HAND PRACTICE

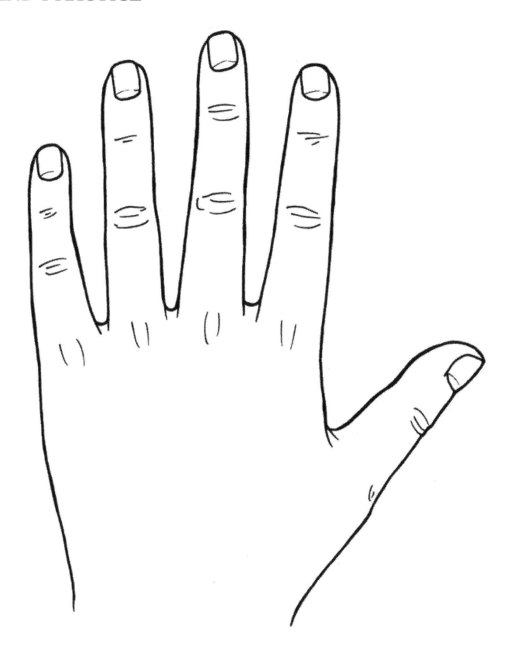

The practical side also has a square shape of the palm, but the fingers are longer and better than those that belong to the side of the base. D'arpentigny says practical hand "square or useful"."The skin is not as rough on practical hands as on the hands of the floor, and there are several rows on the palm. People with practical hands can turn to anything, so this form is called "practical"."They respect credibility and are conservative in terms of perspective. They are disciplined and predictable conformists who hold their feet firmly on the ground. They are attentive, reliable and tidy.

MANUAL SPRAYING

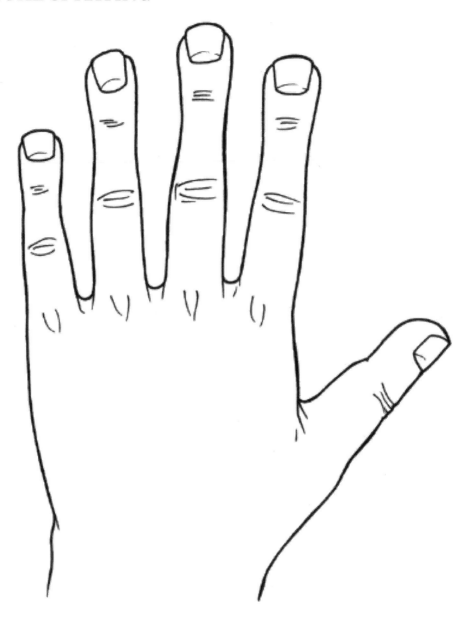

This hand is similar to the practical hand, but the fingertips resemble a spatula, and rockets at the ends of the arpentigny call these hands "spray or active". People with sprayed hands are energetic, persistent and independent. They are ready to work until their efforts are rewarded. Sometimes they are overworked and prefer quantity to quality, in all things.

CONICAL HAND

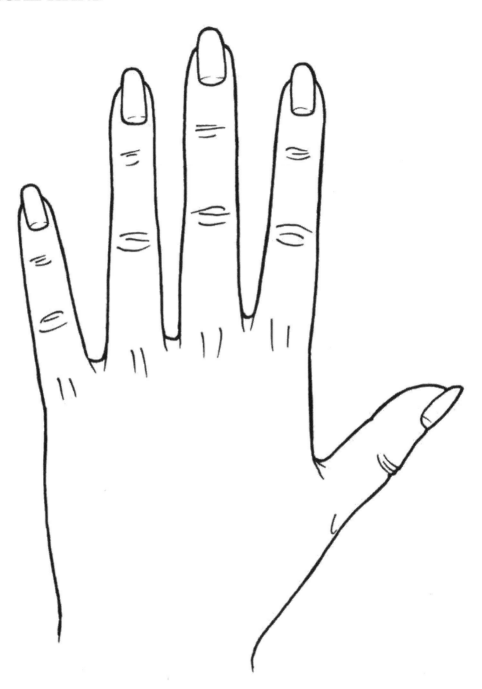

The tapered hand is smooth, curved and attractive in appearance. The palm is slightly elongated, and the fingers are long with rounded tips. The palm tends to be fleshy. People with conical hands are creative, aesthetic and looking for the perfect world. They do not like rudeness of any kind. You have a desire to succeed, but usually you prefer to dream of success, rather than doing the work necessary for any success.

PSYCHIC HAND

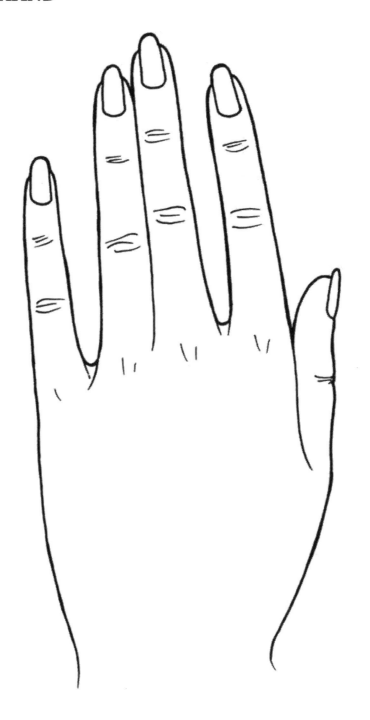

Psychichands are long, thin and elegant. This is very attractive, but fundamentally impossible, because these people spend most of their time in the world fleeing the reality of life. These people are idealistic and very intuitive. They are also sensitive, affectionate and easily vulnerable. The mental hand is an extreme form of watery hand.

THE PHILOSOPHICAL HAND

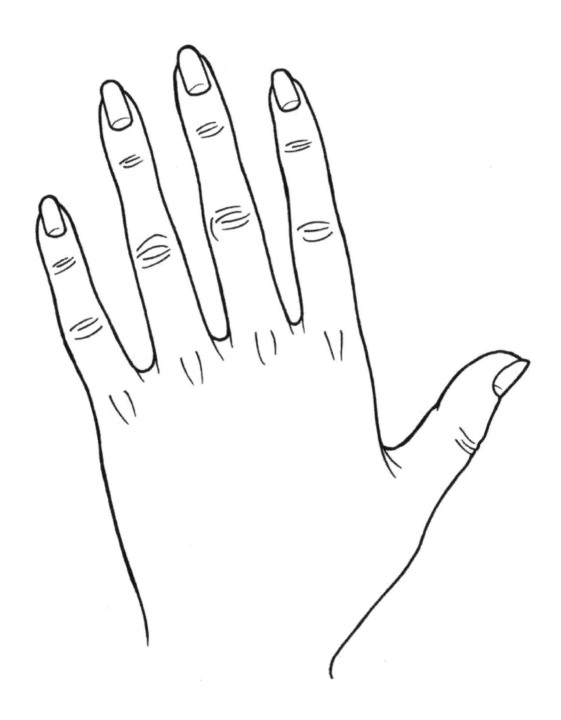

The philosophical hand is square and has long fingers with pointed wrists(Fig. below for this reason, philosophical hands are often called "knotted hands"."These people like to analyze everything carefully before they act. In my classes, I told my students that they imagine thoughts that come through my fingers, reach the first wrist, and walk around and around before moving on to the other wrist, where the process is repeated. Therefore, when a thought reaches the palm, it is carefully analyzed. This is why people with philosophical hands want to know the reasons for everyone and prefer to discover things on their own. People with philosophical hands go their own way and don't care what others think of them. Therefore, they are usually unusual and often eccentric.

MIXED HANDMADE

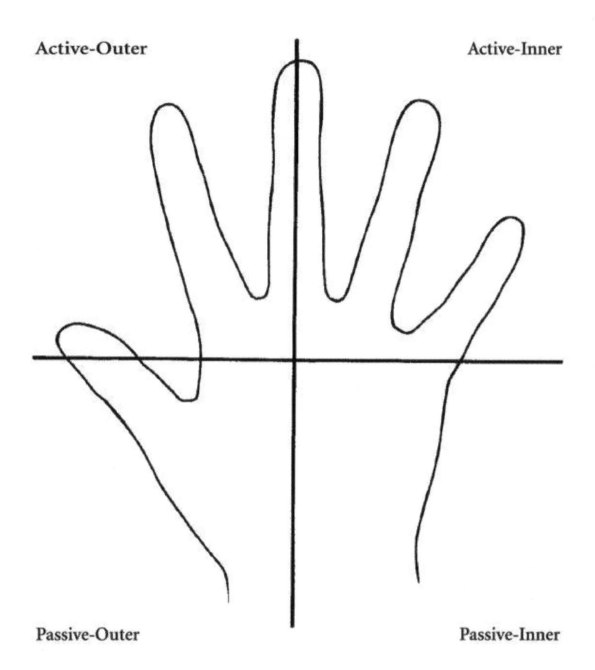

Active-Outer

Active-Inner

Passive-Outer

Passive-Inner

The problem with the D'arpentigny system is that not everyone fits perfectly into one of their classifications. So he had a mixed hand that was used for anyone who had hands that weren't elementary, practical, conical, mental, or philosophical.

Many hands are a mixture of two, three or even four types of Armentine. The palm may be practical, but it has psychic fingers with prominent (philosophical) joints.

In practice, the only real types you are likely to find with the d'arpentigny rating system are people with conical or philosophical hands.

There are many other manual classification systems. Desbarrolles, for example, divided the hands into three groups, mostly based on the shapes of the fingers. No system is perfect. As you have just seen, d'arpentigny had to introduce a "mixed" hand to classify all forms that did not fully correspond to other types. In 1950 George Mucuri has developed a system that divides people into eight groups.1 it's interesting to experiment with different systems, but the first thing we talked about (Earth, Air, Fire, and water) is the one I found most useful and easy to use.

The Four Quadrants

The hand can be divided into four parts with two imaginary lines. The first passes through the Center of the second finger and continues to the wrist. This divides the hand into two halves. The half containing the thumb is the outward pointing part of the hand and refers to what we do in the world. The other half is directed inward and connected to our thoughts.

The second imaginary line begins under the thumb, halfway between the base of the finger and the wrist. This is a horizontal line that crosses the palm of the hand in such a way that it divides the first layer of the line twice. The half of the hand that includes the fingers is active, while the other half is more receptive and passive.

These two lines represent four quadrants: active-external, active-internal, passive-external, and passive-internal. Often when you look at your palm, you notice that one of these four sectors is more noticeable than the others. This may just be a feeling, while in other cases it is clearly more advanced than other dials. If all the numbers look the same, then a person has managed to effectively balance different areas of their life.

Active-External Dialer

The active external dial includes the tip of the thumb and the first finger and half of the second finger. This area is related to the goals and aspirations of a person. If this area is highlighted, the person will put a lot of thought and hard work into achieving their goals. He or she will be excited, energetic, persistent, and impatient.

Passive Set-External

The passive-external dial includes the bottom of the thumb and the hill below it (mount Venus). This area is associated with physical endurance and sexuality. When this zone is well developed, the person will have a lot of energy and stamina, as well as a strong sexual appetite. Conversely, if this area is less developed than other dials, the person will be slightly interested in the exercise and will usually lack enthusiasm and energy.

Active-Internal Set

The active inner dial includes the ring and little finger and half of the other finger. Once this industry is stressful, a person will have an interest in learning and the arts, and it will have little interest in global success.

Passive Set-Internal

The passive-inner quadrant occupies an area known as the mountain of the moon, and is a quarter of the palm located above the thumb. This area is associated with the creative subconscious. When this area is well developed, a person will be endowed with imagination, intuition, sensitivity, and empathy. He or she is probably involved in some form of creativity.

Basic Lines

There are four main lines on the arm: Heart, Head, life and Destiny.

Together they give a vivid picture of the quality of a person's life.

The heart Line provides a clear picture of the emotional and loving life of a person. It reveals emotional energy.

The headline shows how a person thinks. It reveals mental energy.

The lifeline shows how much a person appreciates life and how passionate he is. It reveals physical energy.

The line of destiny gives meaning to human life. This shows that there is something for life and gives the motivation and direction necessary to succeed.

The interaction of these four lines shows exactly how a person uses his emotional, mental and physical feelings. Ideally, all four lines should be clear, well pronounced and deep. Unfortunately, this is more an exception than a rule.

A few years ago, in India, I saw the palms of unconscious people more than a year ago. All the lines disappeared, and the hand seemed strangely empty. In practice, from time to time you will find people with three lines on your hands (heart, head and lifelines). In people who have only two lines, the lines of the heart and head will be interconnected. It's called a monkey, and we'll talk about it later.

In general, the smaller the lines that a person has at hand, the easier it will be to live. This is because most of the lines are caused by nervous tension and anxiety. However, one who has only two or three lines on the palms will lead a boring and monotonous life. In palmistry, we always look for balance. Three lines are too small and hundreds of fine lines of nerve energy are too large.

I think it's better to look at the lines in a certain order. I start with the line of the heart and then the line of the head, the line of life and the line of Destiny. This is because the heart line gives me information about a person's emotional life. In defining this, I turn to a title that speaks to me of human intelligence. After that, I look at the lifeline, which is actually the most important line at hand. It tells me about a person's stamina and energy. Finally, the line of fate tells me his life path. I am gradually superimposing the image of a holistic person, advancing along these lines.

HEART LINE

The heart line is the main line that crosses the palm closest to the fingers. It starts from the side of the palm under the little finger, continues over the entire hand and ends in the area of the first or second finger.

The heart line can bend or stay quite straight at the end. The heart line that bends at the end is called the physical heart line. This line ends at the bottom of the first two fingers or, more often, somewhere in the middle.

PHYSICAL LINE OF THE HEART

People with a physical heart line are relatively easy to express their deeper needs and feelings. They express themselves confidently and affirmatively. When something goes wrong, they are quickly taken in hand and continue to live their lives.

Another type of cardiac line is called the mental cardiac line. It passes through the palm of your hand and does not bend at the fingertips at the end. People with this type of heart line have a harder time expressing their deepest feelings and often have to say that they love and want them. They are sensitive and easily vulnerable. They tend to hide their feelings and suffer peacefully rather than arrange scenes.

In any case, the physical line of the heart is active, and the mental line of the heart is reactive.

A few years ago, someone told me that people with mental heart lines need soft music, candles and wine, and the back seat of an old car is all that people with physical heart lines need. This is certainly an exaggeration, but it gives an idea of the difference between these two types of heart lines. Obviously, from a compatibility point of view, it's easier if two partners have similar heart lines ending in one place.

The heart line is tied to the heart of a person and tied to his physical well-being. Of course, emotional ups and downs can affect a person's physical body. The line of the heart is also closely tied to the soul, because the ability to love and be loved is tied to the divine.

Heart Line Ending Under the First Finger

The final position of this line is important. If the line of the heart ends under the first finger, the person is too idealistic, and he is likely to feel disappointed and disappointed at times by the actions of others. When the line of the heart ends under the second finger, the person will take care only of his own needs and will not have much interest in the needs of others. This person will have a lack of emotional involvement.

Heart Line Ending Under the Second Finger

The simplest position for the heart line at the end is between the first and second fingers. This creates a balance between extreme idealism and selfishness. This person will take care of his own needs, but will also be interested in the needs of others. He or she will also look realistic and keep both feet firmly on the floor.

Heart line ending between first and second fingers

Some people have a heart line that splits in half towards the end. This means that the person has physical and mental qualities heart lines. As a result, he or she will have a complex emotional nature. People with a fork at the end of the heart line are able to see opposite views.

Occasionally you will find a heart line that splits into three lines at the end. This is known as a "trident."It has no specific meaning, but usually designates a lucky life. However, I noticed that this is only the case when the person is in a strong, close and stable relationship.

The heart line should be smooth and well-marked along its entire length. Unfortunately, this is extremely rare. The heart line reflects our emotional life, and we all have ups and downs sometimes. These are revealed on the heart line as "islands", or small ovals that seem to weave. Sometimes they are considered "chains"."They indicate the moments of emotional tension in the person's life when nothing went well. These are usually relationship problems. As a result, it is easy to see if someone has had a bad relationship followed by a good one. The heart line will be full of islands at the time of the difficult relationship, but it will become clear once the person has entered the happy relationship.

A single island on the heart line is a sign of depression at the indicated time. Crosses and pauses on the line indicate a moment of emotional loss. This usually marks the end of a relationship, which could mean a separation or the death of the partner.

A strong, well-marked, deep, and reasonably clear heart line shows that the person will be fundamentally happy and enjoy a fruitful and stable emotional life.

Often you will find a short thin line parallel to the heart line at the end. This is a very lucky sign, showing that the person will benefit from a lasting relationship that is always there, in his old age. Since many people worry about being alone in their old age, I always report it every time I see it in a palm.

All about the Head Line on Your Palm

The head line is probably one of the main features of the hand and immediately refers to his imagination and emotional states. Head line is definitely regarded as one of the most revealing lines between the fingers, because you can get directly and in-depth look at all and who may be researching this line. Your frontline should be present on the right and left palms. If you are really right-handed or a woman, then your right hand means your current state. In these circumstances, the left palm means what you have been blessed with. If you are left-handed, then the opposite is true.

This line is usually a horizontal line that runs through the center of the hand. It should start just above the line of your life and just below your heart. Introduces you to the overall view of your own values, thoughts, train of thought, the brain, thinking and how you approach problems and people as part of your everyday life.

For those who have a line head, which is attached to Your life line at the beginning of the palm of his hand, it means that you have very strong thoughts and your ideas rule over your body instead of the other way. It is not enough to" monitor the flow", the minimum is not so much at the beginning of your everyday life. Your childhood was perhaps very cautious, and most of the time you were probably frightened or temporary.

Along the entire length of the line and even the line, indicate the number of the thing about its existence. The first third of this number represents your youth or when you were younger, to the central part of your line represents your daily life, an adult, and the last part of your line symbolizes you when you are developing in an older person or you reach the last phase of his life.

If your front line is extremely deep or strong, it means that you are very sensitive and therefore incredibly deep in their thoughts. The straighter the line, the more logical you are and how you approach everyday life. This can also mean that you have a very strong and pronounced memory and do not neglect things very quickly. However, in the event that you own a quick line or rather light line, this may indicate that simply you don't go deep into their thoughts. Your thoughts are much more about surface and light, rather than philosophical.

Many people have two or two front lines that are relatively parallel to each other. This is not an extremely widespread feature and usually means that this individual has strong mental abilities or great potential.

This individual is most likely a genius or someone who is absolutely incredibly efficient adapted to the academic or higher educational activities.

In the event that you own a head line fork, it is called a writers fork. He is present in people who might have really colorful and ingenious ideas and who might be a wonderful author. However, the attributes of this line are manifested not only in writing, but can indicate genius and creativity in the choice of other areas. This might indicate that the individual is in fact an incredibly innovative salesman, excellent attorney or an innovative entrepreneur.

Palmistry Lines Reading

Unfortunately, palmistry lines have had a very bad name over the years. Charlatans took advantage of people's need for information and promised to tell them the future, of course, for money.

Such behavior casts a big shadow on the art of reading by hand, so people think that the art form is a scam and how to steal people - instead of understanding that some bad people did it.

I want to be in this article, clarify what you can and can not do palmistry lines and how you can use the information you can provide. We will make a very different separation between myths and reality. Just give a few moments of reading and you will definitely fall in love with this art and advice.

Lines and Relations of Palmistry

People go to the media and readers to understand their soul mate-who he will be, what they will look like and when it will happen.

Reading palmistry can not tell you who this person will be or when exactly you will meet him. However, the leadership that he can give you is no less powerful.

Through the palmistry wedding line and the heart line, you can indicate, what characteristics you should look for in your partner. How they will be related to your personality type. This may indicate a certain stage of life, when it will most likely appear, and how past and future relationships are built as a person.

No need to know who exactly is a real match, palmistry can help you know what is best for you, for a successful relationship and marriage.

Palmistry and Health Lines

The first question people ask themselves when they are going to die. Palmistry, of course, can not be said. Instead, reading The Life Line and The Mercury line, this may indicate general well - being, tendencies to certain diseases and it is recommended to change your life, to make the most of your well-being.

By matching other palmistry lines, you can look at how other aspects of your life, such as relationships and work would make a difference on your well-being, so you can avoid obstacles, or enjoy them if they are positive.

Knowing what you can and should do to make the most of your health life is all you need. It gives you strength.

Lines of Palmistry and Professional Life

The work of your dreams, your next promotion, or what you should study after are not possible answers reading palmistry can provide. Nobody knows.

However, knowing your strengths can lead you in the right direction. Head Analysis, for example, can provide an interesting insight into how your mind works. It can convey whether you are more linear and practical, or more creative. Your ability to see things from different angles. If your reasoning is intact. It can help you understand your chances of successfully working with other people in the group or if you should make a separate trip.

If you are more aware of these trends, it can help you make better decisions and better control success. Neglect her and blindly the unknown.

Palmistry Lines Can Provide Tools, Not A Window, For The Future!

The list could go on, for every aspect of your life. Divination by hand lines I can not say exactly what will happen, but no other method could. The good thing about palmistry is that it provides real tools and advice and, most importantly, gives you control of your life.

Making the right decisions is almost everything in life. But it will be more difficult for you to understand what the right decision is, if you do not have enough impartial knowledge. Reading the lines of palmistry is this knowledge.

But you must understand that palm reading is not entirely true. It's not a guarantee. You can learn, but the responsibility for your life is in your hands. Do not let anyone, however convincing, take control of you.

And this is only the beginning!!!!!

Psychic Readings by Phone - What Type Will Help You?

There are many types of mental readings. When you turn to a psychologist, you should have a basic knowledge of the different types of reading so that you know that one might be more suited to your questions and concerns. You can get psychic readings by phone, in person or via the Internet. With the good psyche you're in, it doesn't have to be a factor in getting a good read.

Almost all psychic readings can be done on the phone. One of the most popular types of telephone psychic readings is tarot reading. When you get reading a Tarot card, you are concentrating your energy on the cards and the psychics read it. Your reading depends on which cards come out and in which position they are located. Tarot Cards are usually made up of 58 cards.

Astrological reading depends on the position of the planets and stars. Most people know their astrological sign and are familiar with horoscopes. Reading astrology go further. Giving a birth date is the first step towards getting an astrology reading. There are several types of astrological readings, including Chinese, Indian and Western astrology.

Numerology is another type of mental reading that is easy to do on the phone. When you talk to the numerologist, he will also ask you for your date of birth. It will then use the numbers associated with the date of birth to determine the number associated with the person. From there, he can deepen your future.

A palm reader can tell a lot about your personality by looking at the palm of your hand. To give you a reading, he will look at The Shape of the hands and fingers and the length and depth of the lines in your hands. The life line and other lines reveal his personality and give the key to his future. The life line shows how long you will live, the heart line defines your love life, and the head line gives you an idea of your personality. There are many other lines like Destiny Line, Health Line, Silver Line and marriage line.

Palmistry Finger Lines - What This Reading Can Do For You

Palmistry finger lines have been abused over the years and that is why some people do not trust them. It is very important not to misinterpret this art because there are things that you can do for yourself and for others that you cannot. this piece will expose the myths and realities of palmistry so you can know what you can do for yourself and what you cannot.

Many people are eager to know who their life partners will be, how they will look and when they will meet them. Unfortunately, palmistry cannot reveal this to you, but it can guide you appropriately. Marriage and heart lines will indicate the traits that you should keep in mind in your partner that matches your personality type. You can predict a specific stage of your life when you can meet him or her. It will help you know the best things to keep in mind so that you will be able to have a successful relationship and marriage.

Palmistry cannot tell you when you will die, but it will guide you to live a healthy life. Through the lifeline, you will be able to know your general well-being and predisposition to certain diseases with recommendation for lifestyle adjustment so that you can improve your state of Health. It will also reveal how other areas of your life, such as work and relationship, could affect your well-being to stay away from obstacles or take advantage of them if they are positive. If you know what to do to improve your health, the power to live long would be in your hand.

Palmistry cannot reveal the work of your dreams, when you will be promoted or what course to study. The head and money line can reveal how your mind works and you will know if you are creative, practical, linear, etc. this will help you know your chances of working in a group or alone. Knowledge of such facts will help you make better decisions that will increase your earning potential and your success rate.

Palmistry finger lines have the ability to provide tools for the future, and not a window for the future. There is a guide for every aspect of life as there are lines for almost every aspect of life. The tools and guidance you get will help you take control of your life. The right decisions need to be made in life, and you may have difficulty trying to find out the right decision if you do not have enough impartial knowledge about yourself. Palmistry lines will give you that knowledge and you can make life decisions with ease.

However, it is important to note that palm reading does not come with a guarantee, but you can learn from it. Your life responsibility is in your hands and the way you handle it will determine what you get out of life.

Palmistry: A Universal Science of Prediction

The art of palmistry is considered to have begun in the period of about 3000 BC. NL ancient China. In India, many scientists have found the presence of the practice of reading palm trees in various Indian fonts that belong to 500. B. No. palmistry began in ancient China gained popularity with the passage of time, and then spread to almost all parts of the world. In the world of palmistry, some names are considered historical and modernizing. Aristotle, Alexander The Great, Hippocrates, smell, etc. they are some of the biggest names in the palmistry area. Among them, Chiero who wrote several books on palmistry was defined by the title 'Father of palmistry'.

Palmistry is more universal form of astrology, more than astrology, which is limited and has adopted a certain religion or tradition. Reading from the palm is carried out on the basis of the study of the palm, which is carried out by Palmistry experts, who are also called palm readers, palmists, hand readers, hand analysts, etc.. The art of palmistry is not only confined to the Hindu or Indian traditions, but it is just a popular among all parts of the world, but with some cultural differences, but the soul itself.

Palmistry: reflection of the past, present and future

Palmistry, as defined, consists in making predictions based on the study of a person's Palm. The study of the palm involves the study of various aspects of the palm. This significantly involves reading the rows of the Palm both in the inner part and those protruding from the outside. In addition to the lines, palmistry also involves with regard to the shape of hand, shape of fingers, skin tone, the supports, the formation of the fingers, the imposition of the fingers and the hair on hand, etc. Palmistovi always manage to consider all these aspects, than comes to the conclusion about a person's life.

Palm reading: read the lines on the palm

More precisely, lines on a palm can specifically call a Life line, Heart line, Destiny line, marriage line, etc. palmistry believes that each individual in this world has a different palm with rare palm lines, and therefore everyone is made to live a different life, even if it is in the light.

To get into the details, each individual has a total of seven primary lines and twelve secondary lines. Each of the seven primary lines fully represents the line of life, line of head, line of heart, line of fate, line of health, line of marriage and the line of sun or line of Apollo. As the name suggests, each of these lines represents a certain aspect of an individual's life, and thus palmistry involves the examination of these lines individually and mutually to get results of certain aspects of life, but also life as a whole. The list of secondary lines includes the Ring of Jupiter, Mars, the Ring of Saturn, Ring of Sun, the girdle of Venus, the Moon, the line of influence, a number of shift, the line of children, the bracelets, the random line and the line to the top.

Given these lines, palmistova considers the thickness of lines, shape of lines, length of lines, the purity of the lines, etc. on the basis of these aspects of the lines, as well as on the basis of the nature of the media in the palm of your hand, the texture of skin, Shape of fingers, etc., palmista is able to adapt to the rules of palmistry or palm reading, and then, is able to draw predictions for the future of the individual.

How to Use Basic Palmistry to Control and Understand Life

Divination use side lines, pencils, and palm marks to connect the intentions of our heart with the reasoning of our mind. They give us a step-by-step snapshot of a person's life from birth to death. Palmistry has nothing to do with world events, the environment, or other external conditions of this kind. Understanding the basics of Palmistry can give us some degree of control over our lives.

You will also notice a person's health, nutrition, daily life meetings, and many other internal perspectives. These templates are formed from files on the hand, matches, or various other symbols. The more a person understands the message in their palms, the more control they will have over their life. Our hands are a reflection of our soul, talking to us for themselves.

Some of the major lines of the palm line of Life, line of heart, line of fate, line of head, line of Sun, line of mercury.

Life line

The waist is considered the most important and highest line of the arm. It predicts not only our longevity, but also other important aspects of our lives. The main aspect that this line shows is the life force and vital energy of the person.

The greater the length and strength of the life line, the greater the passion, vitality, and unity in a person's life. The gap in most of the lines present in the hands can be read as devastating, but on the life line it can mean a complete lifestyle change, such as a new career, home, or new perspective .

Other information that can be collected concerns the physical Constitution and strength of people, as well as the likely flow of their lives.

Heart line

The heart line is more commonly known as the creative curve and represents a person's emotional life. It acts as a guide to people's emotions. It can also indicate whether a person is reserved and cold or warm and gives. Because emotions are the experience of our creative self, they are constantly changing or fluctuating.

Cold temperatures in people are given if the heart line is long and straight. This line is considered a record of the physical state of the heart and the emotional state of the mind.

The smallest fragmented fine lines of the main line of the heart indicate an emotional break caused by fear and fatigue.

Line of destiny

The fatal line is also known as the career line or the Saturn line. The Fate line also provides information about career and employment prospects. Achieving our goals and a decent standard of living are aspects that depend on the power of fate.

The head line

The main role describes our mental abilities and intellectual strength. This line also shows the scope and depth of human thought, career potential, memory, and attributes of human common sense. Ideally, it can only be found sparsely and slightly curved in the center.

Sun line

The sun line, also known as the Apollo line, will be the second fatal line. A strong solar line is considered favorable and can compensate for a weak death line. The presence of a solar line strengthens the fatal line.

Mercury Line

The mercury line is known as the human health line. Lying under the fourth finger. The perfect line of mercury comes from mount Neptune. This suggests that there is an ideal digestion, and the functioning of the stomach allows you to have a good time in the intestines, keeping a clear head and rich energy as the main characteristics necessary for a business meeting. It is more profitable to have a missing health line.

From the moment we are born, we carry the map of our life in our hands. These maps contain power templates. They are a record of our life before death. Using this map, basic palmistry and our gift of free will can become masters of our destiny.

The Life Line

The Lifeline provides information about the physical well - being, health and endurance of a person. It also shows with what enthusiasm a person treats his life.

There are more misunderstandings in this line than any other aspect of palmistry. I could not even calculate how many times people asked me so short life path of their son or daughter, who will die young. In fact, the Lifeline has little or no relation to life expectancy, and short lifelines are usually stretched as characters.

The lifeline shows the degree of vitality and energy that a person possesses at any time in his life. It also shows how much a person is full of enthusiasm and passion. As a result, it is closely related to the degree of satisfaction that a person gets from life.

Although I do not read this line first, this is by far the most important point because it clearly shows how much life and energy a person possesses at every stage of his life.

The line of life begins from the side of the hand between Jupiter (the first) finger and thumb. Then the semicircle bypasses the thumb, ends at the bottom of the palm, near the wrist.

The life line passes well through the palm of the hand (energy)

The amount of area surrounding it is important. A life line that crosses the palm well shows someone with a lot of stamina and energy. This person will be adventurous, venture out, and enjoy every opportunity. The lifeline next to the fingers belongs to someone who is half-alive, apathetic, and lacking energy and enthusiasm.

That's lifeline embraces thumb (lack of energy)

A raised crowd surrounded by a life line is known as Mount Venus and determines how passionate man is. The breast should be raised and feel a little tight to the touch. The more it will be, the more passionate the person will be. If the sponge is to the touch, the person will be interested in sensual pleasures and exaggerated whenever the opportunity arises.

Worry About the Line

I saw a whipped Venus upside down. People with such education are not interested in sex and usually do not like people of the opposite sex. They tend to be cold and useless.

The initial position of the life line is important. In most people, it starts halfway between the base of the first finger and thumb. (This is, by the way, the ideal position to start, because in palmistry, we are always looking for a balance.) If the life line begins closer to the first finger than that, the person will be ambitious and determined to achieve his goals. This property becomes more pronounced as close as possible to the line of life, starting with the first finger. On the contrary, if the life line begins near the thumb, a person will not have ambitions and will accept life exactly as it comes.

The life line itself must be deep, clear and clearly indicated. Someone with such a line will appreciate good health and will be passionate about life. Most lifelines are a mix. The line can be well labeled for a part of its length, then slightly weaker before it becomes strong again. The period of weakness indicates the time when a person's energy levels were below normal. It was probably a period of bad health.

The islands on the life line show depression at certain times. They can also indicate a period of hospitalization. A chained life path is a sign of many health problems, usually of an emotional nature.

Interruptions of life lines are common and are usually periods when a person changes his view of life. Sometimes, however, these interruptions can be dramatic and are usually caused by a breakup or a health problem. Usually, each break will be covered by a line overlap, which provides a form of protection at a specific time. The overlap becomes a small "sister of the line."

Sister Line

The sister line is a thin line on the thumb side of the waist line (the image below is called Sister line because it is parallel to the waist line, it actually becomes a "sister" for her. It is also known as the line of Mars. Some people have a sister line that covers the entire length of the life line. However, it is usually located at the beginning of the life line that embraces growth. The sister line is a bit like two life lines and provides additional protection for a person at a specific time. For example, if someone has a sister line up to the end of their life line, that person will be protected later in life and will not end up falling or being incompetent. Online nurse is always happy to see on the arm.

The Timing in Hand

For thousands of years, palmists have discussed how time events in hand. I remember a lively discussion I had with several palmists in New Delhi Thirty years ago, during which one gave another a black eye as they discussed how the events of the time. The rest of us agreed to differ, as we all had different ideas on the subject. In fact, there are a number of fundamental differences between Eastern and Western palmistry, and they were just as surprised to learn how I programmed events in one hand as I had to learn their methods.

In practice, you should look at both hands to determine the timing of important events. It is better that you can detect an important event that happened to the person in the past, and then measure back and forth from that date.

Unfortunately, there is no automatic method that works every time. During my practice, I experienced all the methods described here.

However, I also use my intuition. I think it's possible to become a capable palm reader without using any intuition. However, if you want to become an outstanding palmist, you need to trust and act according to your intuition.

I have a good example. Many years ago, shortly after becoming a professional palmist, I was invited to read the palms of all the guests at a private party. I really like this guy's reservations. The atmosphere is nice and relaxed, and I have the opportunity to examine many hands during the night.

Unfortunately, that night I didn't feel well, and I came to the party with a headache. They put me in a dark corner to do the readings. I learned to be ready for any eventuality, and I had a flashlight and a magnifying glass with me.

However, when I started the first reading, I discovered that the concentration required aggravated my headache. I thought I'd never spend the night, but, much faster than I expected, I'd read Everyone's palms, and I'd come home. I managed to get rid of the headaches in my dream.

The next morning, the lady who organized the party called me. I was excited about the readings I gave. Apparently, he had been incredibly accurate and accurate about the events that had occurred in the past, and everyone had been extremely impressed. I was surprised. The whole night had been a total blur for me. I couldn't concentrate and concentrate, and I had done all the reading saying the first thing that came to mind.

Obviously, I agreed with my intuition, and in doing so, I had given better than usual, even with a strong headache. Since then, I've always said everything that comes to mind, even if it doesn't make sense to me. I can tell the client it's an intuitive flash, not something you see in your palms. However, as I hold and examine his hands, it is quite possible that he will receive the information through some kind of psychometry.

It takes a lot of practice to be good at the time of events, on the one hand. Be patient. Try all the methods described here. Ask your customers questions to determine how accurate you are. Gradually, you will find that sometimes become better and better events in the hands of your customers.

Be careful of anyone who claims to be able to determine the month and day of a particular event. It is quite difficult to accurately determine the year, and it is impossible to determine the day and month without using intuition. William G. Benham wrote: "There are some who can count an event and set the time in a year, but those who have achieved such a skill are few. Others succeed in two, three or five years. No one can do more than fix the year in which such an event occurs, if it is completely based on the rules of palmistry.

DESTINY LINE

The easiest way to determine time is by far to use the target line (figure 31). It takes the first thirty-five years of a person's life to the line of destiny to reach the line of the head. It takes the next fourteen years to reach the heart line (at the age of forty-nine), and the rest of life is taken with any part of the target line remains. Accordingly, the first part of the target line, to the extent that it meets the head line, can be divided into three, giving the approximate age of twelve and twenty-four years. Similarly, the section between the lines of the head and heart can be divided in half, to give the age of forty-two years.

It may seem strange that the first thirty-five years of life occupy most of the line of Destiny. This is because this is the time when we are growing up and working on what we want to do with our lives. At the age of thirty-five, most people have a fairly good idea of what they want to do. However, I have an eighty-three-year-old friend who is still trying to figure out what he wants to do with his life!

Between thirty-five and forty-nine years, the person follows a reliable path. You risk being in a permanent relationship and advancement in a career. Of course, if this is not the case, there will be changes in the target line between the head and the heart lines.

It may seem strange that most people's destination lines stop around the age of forty-nine. This certainly does not mean that they do not have a destiny after this age. All this means that most people are on their way at this time, and, accordingly, there are no major changes in their direction in the fifties, sixties or sixties.

People with a line of destiny that goes far beyond the line of the heart will experience new and different activities in old age. This could be a sign of a late departure, in many cases. This is often a sign of longevity.

Your Hands Can Define Your Future

Your hands not only aid you in your daily lives with absolutely everything, but they also predict your future. Palmistry is the divine art of studying people's hands - the texture, color and shape of the palm, length of the fingers and lines that run across your hands.

Hidden within these lines lie the secrets to your future. Your hands are capable of answering all the baffling questions under the guidance of right seers. These seers are also called palmists, palm readers.

Palmistry has been believed to be discovered in the Hindu culture. From India, it spread far and wide to China, Tibet, Egypt, Persia, and various European countries. However, with the coming of the Renaissance Age, scholars of those times classified palmistry under several forbidden arts and it was almost wiped out.

Experts have classified palm reading into two sections-

• Chiromancy- the study of lines on your hands, and

• Chirognomy- the study of the shape, color and texture of your hands.

It is important for us to know the many different styles of palm reading. One school of palmists studies the palm that is not dominant. This means that if you are a right-handed person, the lines on the left hand are read and if you are left-handed, then the right hand is read. Another school of palmists choose to read the dominant hand since the other one is considered to be in a state of sub consciousness.

It is not only the lines that are at the core of palm reading, but the choice of the hand and it's shape itself. Let's see how...

- The left hand is believed to be controlled by the right side of the brain which makes it a possessor of relationships, compassion and understanding. It reflects the natural, inner self of the person.
- The right hand is believed to be controlled by the left side of the brain which means it has the abilities of logic, reasoning and language. It reflects the objective, outer self of the person.

Your hands are further divided into four segments after the four elements of nature- earth, fire, water and air.

It is considered to be earth if you have a square palm with thick fingers. Air hands have long fingers and rectangular palms. Water hands have an oval palm with long, conical fingers. And lastly, fire hands have a square, pink palm with short fingers.

Now we will move on to the three most important and commonly read lines by palmists' world across.

- The heart line represents your heart both physically and metaphorically. It can give you an insight into your emotional stability, cardiac health, romance and depression.
- The head line interprets your creativity and analytical skills. It can decode your learning methods, thirst for knowledge and communication skills.
- The life line, as the name suggests helps you understand any out of the ordinary event that could happen in your lives. Whether it is any big physical injury, or some incident that could have a big effect on you, and even the possibility of a permanent relocation.

Your palms hold a lot of other secrets which can be revealed to you if you are really looking for them. But you must always remember that while they have the power to predict the future, these very palms can aid you in shaping your future the way you like it.

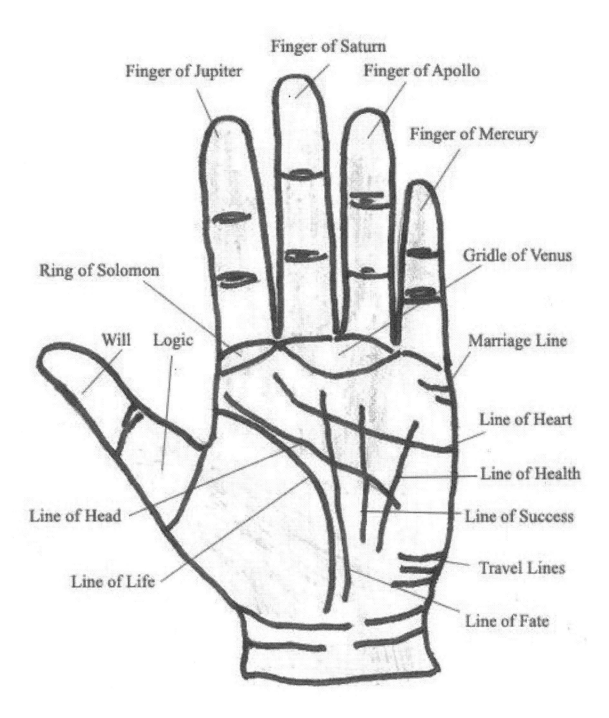

Kind reader,

Thank you very much, I hope you enjoyed the book.

Can I ask you a big favor?

I would be grateful if you would please take a few minutes to leave me a gold star on Amazon.

Thank you again for your support.

Rebecca Hood

Printed in Great Britain
by Amazon